Structures in the Arctic

WRITTEN BY
Ibi Kaslik

Published by Inhabit Education | www.inhabiteducation.com

Inhabit Education (Iqaluit), P.O. Box 2129, Iqaluit, Nunavut, X0A 1H0
(Toronto), 191 Eglinton Avenue East, Suite 302, Toronto, Ontario, M4P 1K1

Printed in Canada.

ISBN: 978-1-77266-085-2

There are many different
types of structures
in the world around us.
Let's look at a few together!

This is an igloo.
Igloo means “snow house.”
It is made of blocks of
ice and snow.

BIRD HOUSE
COOPER
ISLAND

This is a hunting camp.
It is set up on the land for
hunting and fishing.
The cabin is made from
wood and metal.

This is a snowmobile.
It can glide fast on ice
and snow.

People in the North
use snowmobiles to travel
to places without roads.

ARCTIC CAT
CROSSFIRE
8

This is a house.
It is built on stilts
because the ground is
always frozen.

This is an airport.
People come here when
they need to travel to
the South or to another
community.

The airport in Iqaluit
is bright yellow.

IQALUIT
ᐃᖃᓗᐃᑦ
Do not enter
Entrée interdite
Enter
Entrée